Hidden Treasure for Little Minds™

Daily Devotions for 2 to 6 Year Olds

Adesola Obunge

AuthorHouse™
1663 Liberty Drive
Bloomington, IN 47403
www.authorhouse.com
Phone: 1-800-839-8640

Author copyright © 2011 by. Adesola Obunge. All rights reserved.

Cover and interior illustrations copyright © 2010 by Jonathan Harper. All rights reserved.

Scripture quotations marked NLT are taken from the Holy Bible, New Living Translation, copyright ©1996, 2004. Used by permission of Tyndale House Publishers, Inc., Wheaton, Illinois 60189. All rights reserved.

Scripture quotations marked NIV are taken from the Holy Bible, New International Version®, copyright ©1973, 1978, 1984 by International Bible Society. Used by permission of Zondervan Publishing House. All rights reserved.

Scripture quotations marked CEV are taken from the Holy Bible, Contemporary English Version, copyright ©1995. Used by permission of American Bible Society. All rights reserved.

Scripture quotations marked KJV are taken from the Holy Bible, King James Version. Public Domain.

No part of this book may be reproduced, stored in a retrieval system, or transmitted by any means without the written permission of the author.

First published by AuthorHouse 1/5/2011

ISBN: 978-1-4490-5372-7

Printed in the United States of America
Bloomington, Indiana

This book is printed on acid-free paper.

This book belongs to

Jakarri Symone Wilson

Given by Kevin Terrell Evans

On the occasion of Just Because

Date Feb 17 2015

Contents — Page Number

1. Celebrate Life 2
2. A Positive Attitude 3
3. Taught Of The Lord 4
4. Give, Give, Give 5
5. Love One Another 6
6. God Is My Source 7
7. God Takes Care of You 8
8. Never Alone 9
9. Praise And Thanks 10
10. Always On Top 11
11. Trust God 12
12. See With The Eyes of Faith 13
13. Angels All Around 14
14. Mighty Mountains 15
15. When You Are Sad, Smile 16
16. Help Is Always Near 17
17. Beautiful Creation 18
18. I Will Say 19
19. A Special Friend 20
20. But I Can't See God 21
21. The Name of The Lord 22
22. Today 23
23. A Wellspring of Joy 24
24. A Super Doctor 25
25. No Weapon 26
26. God's Gifts 27
27. Develop Godly Character 28
28. Think Like God 29
29. Are You Angry? 30
30. You Are Special 31
31. You Have Everything You Need 32
32. Wisdom From Above 33
33. He's Working In You 34
34. Before Day One 35
35. The Purpose of The Book 36
36. Into My Heart 37
37. It All Counts 38
38. You Have What You Say 39
39. So He Thinks, So Is He 40

Contents	Page Number
40 Never Thirsty	41
41 In His Shadow	42
42 Grace	43
43 Talk To God, Listen To Him	44
44 Super Strength	45
45 More Than Enough	46
46 Singing Psalms And Hyms	47
47 Give God First Place	48
48 Thank You	49
49 I Am Happy And I Know It	50
50 I Want More	51
Do you know Jesus?	52

Preface
(Author's Note to Parents & Guardians)

We live in an age where children learn much quicker than previous generations, and when so many "suggestions" are being put before their eyes and ears by various forms of media. However, as a parent or guardian, it is your responsibility to guard the heart of your child by determining what is fed in. There is a lot you can do to train your child to live wisely in their generation. My experience as a mother has taught me that it is a time to build the truth and life into your child, laying a good foundation in the very early stages.

The word of God is never too advanced; it really is simple and explains itself to babes. So help your child to set a desired length of time depending on his or her age, but be sure to make devotional times a consistent and daily practice.

These 'easy-to-do' daily devotions will help you:
- Introduce biblical principles and the right values from an early age
- Share a scripture verse with your child
- Teach your child about only speaking what is good or desired
- Have a consistent time out together everyday
- Train your child on the need to seek God for him or herself daily
- Keep your child's attention focused for up to 10 minutes
- Get your child asking questions about putting their faith in God

I hope your child finds this devotional book exciting as he or she enjoys the colour and vibrancy on the book pages, whilst exploring what God has to say about living right in these times.

Dear Little One,

Welcome to your book of daily devotions. My name is Adesola and I wrote this book to help you learn about God and spend time with Him every day.

☺ God is real: you can't see Him with your eyes, but you know Him with your heart.

☺ God is the Trinity: He is Father, Son and Holy Spirit. The Father loves and cares for you. The Son is Jesus who came to the earth many years ago and died to save mankind. He went back to heaven, but is coming back soon again to take God's children to heaven with Him. The Holy Spirit is here with you now on earth, as the deposit of a glorious life you will live with God later. He is comforter and speaks to you gently.

☺ God loves you: He is glad that you have come to talk to Him and to read His words to you. God loves to have a good friendship with you and He will be the best friend ever.

I hope you discover many wonderful things about God as you use your book of devotions every day.

God bless you,
Adesola Obunge

Celebrate Life

God wants you to celebrate life everyday. He has given you so many things to enjoy because He loves you and delights in seeing you happy. God sent His son Jesus to give you abundance and overflowing joy.

Can you think of five things to rejoice about? Why don't you talk about them today and celebrate. You can even do a dance or clap your hands to give God thanks for them.

My Confession Today

I put my hope in God. He provides all I need and gives me life.

My Bible Verse

Hope in God, who richly provides us with everything for our enjoyment.
1 Timothy 6:17b (NIV)

A Positive Attitude

Being positive means you expect the best to happen all the time. It is being confident that God's goodness and mercy follow you every day. God wants you to trust Him at all times and no matter what happens, because He will always take care of you.

So make sure you keep good thoughts and choose positive emotions because they will make you to stand out and achieve great things in life.

My Confession Today

I trust you Lord with all my heart and mind. Thank you for taking care of me.

My Bible Verse

Trust in the LORD with all your heart and lean not on your own understanding.
Proverbs 3:5 (NIV)

Taught Of The Lord

You will have many teachers when you go to school. Some may teach you science subjects and others art subjects. But the Holy Spirit is the best teacher.

He will teach you what to do, what to say and how to live. He does this by telling you things that are in the Bible. When you obey the Bible, you will have great peace. One way that you can do what the Bible says is to obey what your dad and mom tell you everyday.

My Confession Today

God teaches me and I obey Him. I have great peace.

My Bible Verse

I will teach all your children, and they will enjoy great peace.
Isaiah 54:13 (NLT)

Give, Give, Give

One day Jesus was talking to lots of men, women and children on a mountain. They were with Him for a long time, so they became hungry. One little boy gave Jesus his lunch so that they could all share it. Jesus thanked God for the fish and bread and asked God to make it more than enough for everyone to eat. All the people ate and they still had twelve baskets full of bread and fish left.

Jesus shows us that we must give. When you give, you are showing love to people. When you give, thank God for making it grow until there is more than enough for you and for others too.

My Confession Today

I love to give and I love to share.

My Bible Verse

You feed them from the abundance of your own house, letting them drink from your river of delights.
Psalm 36:8 (NLT)

Love One Another

Love is the greatest gift in life. Love always gives to others. Love always looks for the best in others. Love always says good things to encourage and build up. Love asks politely. Love says 'please' and 'thank you'. Love is kind. Love thinks good things of others. Love forgives and does not easily become offended. Love rejoices in the truth. Love is always hopeful and never gives up. Love never loses faith.

Today, love somebody by giving them a smile and saying hello.

My Confession Today

God loves me and so I love others.

My Bible Verse

Three things will last forever - faith, hope, and love - and the greatest of these is love.
1 Corinthians 13:13 (NLT)

God Is My Source

God made the whole universe and everything in our world. After He made everything, He created men, women and children. He blessed us and told us that He had already provided all that we could ever need. This means that God is our source.

When you eat your food or drink some water today, be sure to say thank you to God for all the wonderful things He has provided for you.

My Confession Today

I know God has provided all I need. He is my source.

My Bible Verse

The Lord is my Shepherd; I have all that I need. Psalm 23:1 (NLT)

God Takes Care of You

Mom and dad look after you. When you wake up they help you brush your teeth and give you a bath. They give you food when you are hungry. They also talk to you and play with you. Sometimes they take you to the park or you go swimming in the pool. These are some of the many ways that they take care of you.

Did you know that God takes care of you too? He does so by giving you special people like mom, dad, grandparents or teachers that can look after you.

You are very special to God and He loves you.

My Confession Today

God loves me and He takes care of me.

My Bible Verse

Humble yourselves, therefore, under God's mighty hand, that he may lift you up in due time. Cast all your anxiety on him because he cares for you. 1 Peter 5:6-7 (NIV)

Never Alone

Wherever you are, do you know that you are never alone? God is always watching over you to keep and protect you. He has also given His angels to do the same thing. They surround you and help you, so that you don't hurt yourself. They bring good things to you.

The Bible tells us that God's angels camp around us and bear us up. Even though you cannot see them, they are with you always. You are never alone because God protects you.

My Confession Today

God is my security. I am never alone.

My Bible Verse

He will order his angels to protect you wherever you go.
Psalm 91:11 (NLT)

Praise And Thanks

We must be thankful everyday and give praise to God. This is good because it shows that we are happy with all that He provides. What can you be thankful for today? Think about some things that you like: your toys, clothes, story books, the warm sun, the cool breeze in your face, water to swim in and your friends. How about fun days out playing in the park, walking the dog, watering flowers in the garden or nice games like hide and seek?

It is good to tell God you like these things and are happy He gave them to you to enjoy. This is how you praise Him everyday.

My Confession Today

Thank you God, for all the good things that I have.

My Bible Verse

Praise the Lord! Give thanks to the Lord, for he is good! His faithful love endures forever. Who can list the glorious miracles of the Lord? Who can ever praise him enough?
Psalm 106:1-2 (NLT)

Always On Top

You are a winner! God loves to make all His children winners because He is a winner. He helps you to be the best all the time.

When you are at school, at play or doing other things, He sees to it that you triumph. To triumph means to win and to have the victory. You will always win because God helps you.

You will always be on top!

My Confession Today

Thank God who always helps me win.

My Bible Verse

But thanks be to God! He gives us the victory through our Lord Jesus Christ.
1 Corinthians 15:57 (NIV)

Trust God

When you trust someone, it means you believe in them. For example, if your mom or dad tells you that they will buy you a toy or special gift, you know that they will do it. When you sit on a chair, you trust that it won't give way under you. You also know that your parents won't let anything bad happen to you.

It is very important to place the same confidence in God. He always does what He promises to do; so you can trust Him.

My Confession Today

I put my hope in God's holy word.

My Bible Verse

Trust in the Lord with all your heart; do not depend on your own understanding. Seek his will in all you do, and he will show you which path to take
Proverbs 3: 5-6 (NLT)

See With The Eyes of Faith

12

The Bible says that the just will live by faith. A just person is someone who has asked Jesus to come into their heart to save them. Faith means placing confidence and trust in God and His word.

When the children of Israel had to conquer Jericho, God told them to march around the city for seven days and then make a very loud shout on the seventh day. The walls of Jericho fell down because Israel believed God by doing what He told them to do. They saw their victory first, with the eyes of faith.

You must learn to believe that God is real and that the Bible is true. This is how you can see with the eyes of faith.

My Confession Today

The just shall live by faith. I have the faith of God.

My Bible Verse

It is through faith that a righteous person has life.
Romans 1:17 (NLT)

# Angels All Around

God loves you very much, so one of the things He has done is to provide heavenly angels to keep you from harm. They help you every day. Angels were created to serve all of God's children. To get them to work on your behalf, you must speak like God and believe they are around you ready to do what you say. You can't see them with your natural eyes, but you can believe in your heart.

God's angels are commanded to bring good things to you. You have thousands of angels around you.

My Confession Today

The angel of the Lord camps around me and keeps me from trouble.

My Bible Verse

The angel of the Lord is a guard; he surrounds and defends all who fear God.
Psalm 34:7 (NLT)

Mighty Mountains

A mountain is very big and high so it would take a long time to climb to the top. There are many mountains around Jerusalem, the city of God. God is a dear Father who has promised to protect His children just like the mountains that surround Jerusalem give protection to that city. His protection is around you.

Every time you think of mighty mountains or when you see a picture of one in a book, remember that God is protecting you.

My Confession Today

Thank you Lord that I am safe. You keep me like the mountains that surround the city of Jerusalem.

My Bible Verse

Those who trust in the LORD are like Mount Zion, which cannot be shaken but endures forever. As the mountains surround Jerusalem, so the LORD surrounds his people both now and forevermore.
Psalm 125:1-2 (NIV)

When You Are Sad, Smile

Sometimes we all feel sad or worry about something. But the Bible tells us that we must not stay sad or worry about things. This is because we can't change things by ourselves.

One day, Jesus was sad because his friend had died, so He prayed and asked God to raise His friend to life again. Lazarus came to life and his family were very happy to have him back with them.

Anytime you are sad, do what the Bible says: always be full of joy in the Lord. Rejoice! This means you have to tell yourself to cheer up and smile. This also means you have to pray about what you are feeling or what happened. When you tell God, He will make you feel better.

Remember to smile.

My Confession Today

The joy of the Lord is my strength. So I can smile always.

My Bible Verse

Give your burdens to the Lord, and he will take care of you.
Psalm 55:22 (NLT)

Help Is Always Near

16

Do you know who a helper is? A helper is someone who is there to assist another person. When your mom or dad gives you a drink, they are helping you so that you won't be thirsty anymore.

God also helps us. He has given you the Holy Spirit to help you learn more about Him and to tell you what He says. The Holy Spirit also teaches you the truth from the Bible and He helps you to understand.

With the Holy Spirit as your Helper, you will always know what to do to please God, your Father.

My Confession Today

My help comes from God.

My Bible Verse

Our help is from the Lord, who made heaven and earth.
Psalm 124:8 (NLT)

Beautiful Creation

There are so many beautiful things in the world. We have trees with many shapes of leaves, plants and flowers with many bright colours. We have the sea and waves that make wonderful sounds on the beach, and the wind to keep us cool from the heat of the sun. The sun also gives light during the daytime and the moon and stars shine during the night time.

The Bible says that all of creation declares the glory of God and His marvellous works: they speak every day, and without a sound or a word their message goes through all the earth.

What beautiful creation!

My Confession Today

I am fearfully and wonderfully made.

My Bible Verse

The heavens declare the glory of God; the skies proclaim the work of his hands.
Psalm 19:1 (NIV)

I Will Say

God is a place of refuge and strength for those who trust in Him. He provides shelter from the storms of life. Some things may happen and make us sad. When we trust in Him, He gives us light and we do not have to be afraid. Being where God is makes us confident that even if trouble comes, God will hide us in His secret place and put us out of the reach of evil. He is a Rock and High Tower for His children.

Anytime you are afraid remember that God keeps you and say, 'God is my Refuge and my Strength'.

My Confession Today

The Lord is my Refuge and place of Safety. I trust Him.

My Bible Verse

Live under the protection of God Most High and stay in the shadow of God All-Powerful.
Psalm 91:1 (CEV)

A Special Friend

A special friend is someone you really like and are very fond of. You enjoy being with them and doing things together. Can you name some special people in your life? It's really fun having them, isn't it?

Jesus and the Holy Spirit are both very special friends and you can also enjoy being with them. You can read the Bible and talk to them. When you don't know what to do, you can ask them to help you. This is how you spend time with Jesus and the Holy Spirit.

And if you do what the Holy Spirit says, He will continue to tell you God's secrets so that you can live a good life.

My Confession Today

God has sent the Comforter to me. He is the Holy Spirit.

My Bible Verse

You are my friends if you do what I command. John 15:14 (NIV)

But I Can't See God

Can you see air? No, but you can hear the wind blowing. Can you see how day turns into night? No, but you know for sure when it is daytime and when it is night. Can you tell why the sea does not cross its boundary line, but stops at the seashore? Every time the waves rush to the beach, they must return back.

Can you see God? No, not with your physical eyes, but you know that He is everywhere. He made all of creation and the Bible says you must believe that He exists and that He loves to reward those who follow Him diligently.

When you see the next sunset or rainbow, remember that this is God. Yes, you can see Him this way!

My Confession Today

I can't see God, but I know He is real. He shows His love and power in everything He created.

My Bible Verse

It is impossible to please God without faith. Anyone who comes to Him must believe that God exists and that He rewards those who sincerely seek Him.
Hebrews 11:6 (NLT)

The Name of The Lord

What is your name? That's what you are called. A name is what a person is known as. In the Bible, we see that people's names always had a meaning. This described who they were and the role or purpose they would have in life.

God's names also describe who He is. Some of His many names are Mighty One, Everlasting Father, Lily of the Valley, Rock of Ages and Tower of Strength. If you believe in Him, He will become all of this and more to you. He loves to show His power in your life.

My Confession Today

The name of the Lord is my strong tower. I am safe in His presence.

My Bible Verse

The name of the Lord is a strong tower; the righteous run to it and are safe.
Proverbs 18:10 (NIV)

Today

What day of the week is it today? If you don't know, ask your mom or dad. Tomorrow will be a different day of the week, but that does not matter. On each 'TODAY', you have a brand new day that God has given you to enjoy. So whether you're going to school or staying home with your family, you can have all the fun possible.

Each new 'TODAY', God has already provided everything you need. He loves it when you show everyone around that you are glad about 'TODAY'.

My Confession Today

This is the day the Lord has made. I will rejoice and be glad in it.

My Bible Verse

But encourage one another daily, as long as it is called 'TODAY'.
Hebrews 3:13 (NIV)

A Wellspring of Joy

Joy is a gift from God placed in your heart. It does not require good circumstances before it shows up. Even when bad things happen, joy is stronger than sorrow, pain or hurt. It makes you stay calm and it helps you to smile. Joy equals strength.

When you choose joy, then nothing can keep you sad. When someone takes your toy or does not share with you, you can stay happy and go and share with someone else.

Choose joy today. Joy is always inside you.

My Confession Today

The joy of the Lord is my strength.

My Bible Verse

Celebrate. Don't be dejected and sad, for the joy of the Lord is your strength!
Nehemiah 8:10 (NLT)

A Super Doctor

When people get sick they may have to go to the doctor to get some medicine so they can feel better. The Bible says that Jesus is a super doctor. He does more than just giving medicine. His word has the power to heal and to keep you healthy all the time.

Trust that Jesus will keep you well always.

My Confession Today

The word of God is life and health for my body.

My Bible Verse

The word of God brings life to those who find them, and healing to their whole body.
Proverbs 4:22 (NLT)

No Weapon

No weapon formed against you shall prosper. This is a great promise that God has made to you because He loves you so much.

A weapon is a thing used to harm someone, but God wants you to know that nothing can overcome His power. His power is the greatest that ever was and as long as you live under God's protection, He will shield you and will not allow any evil attacks to get the better of your body, mind or any other part of your life.

Surely there will be times in life when you may be in danger, feel weak, be alone, or even have bad thoughts coming to your mind. In these times, you need to trust in God's power.

My Confession Today

God is my refuge and my strength, my present help in times of need.

My Bible Verse

No weapon turned against you will succeed. You will silence every voice raised up to accuse you. These benefits are enjoyed by the servants of the Lord. Isaiah 54:17 (NLT)

God's Gifts

Have you ever given a gift to someone? We give gifts because we have been loved, and now we want to show love to another person.

God has also given each person on earth wonderful gifts and that includes you. He has given you His presence to fill your heart and He has given you His word in the Bible so that you know how to live like Him. In the body of Christ or the church, He has given you brothers and sisters, special teachers and preachers. Others can sing beautifully to praise God and others still, encourage. We all have different gifts, but they are all special. This is so that we can all grow up in His love.

What are the gifts that you have? Thank God for some of the personal gifts that you have today.

My Confession Today

Every good and perfect gift is given to me by God.

My Bible Verse

When he ascended to the heights, he gave gifts to his people so that he might fill the entire universe with himself.
Ephesians 4:8-10 (NLT, paraphrased)

Develop Godly Character

God wants you to be like Him because you are His child. He wants you to look like Him. Look at your mom or dad. Do you look like them? Maybe your eyes or hair are the same colour.

You must learn to always do things the way God does. For example, God is always loving and kind. He wants you to speak kindly to others, to be polite, gentle and to always tell the truth.

This is what it means to be like God and grow in godly character.

My Confession Today

I am God's child so I copy His good behaviour.

My Bible Verse

Love is patient and kind.
1 Corinthians 13:4 (NLT)

Think Like God

On each day that comes there are many new things to learn. Everyone is always learning. Babies grow and then learn how to crawl or walk or to feed themselves and grown ups learn new skills at their jobs.

The Bible says that the most important thing we all need to do is to learn how to think in a good way all the time. Thinking good thoughts leads to saying good things, and then doing or having good things. When we read and think about what God says in the Bible, then we can change our thoughts to match His *higher thoughts*.

These *higher thoughts* mean that your mind is renewed and you are changed into a new person. God's *higher thoughts* lead to a prosperous and successful life.

My Confession Today

My mind is renewed by God's word daily.

My Bible Verse

Instead, let the Spirit renew your thoughts and attitudes.
Ephesians 4:23 (NLT)

Are You Angry?

When you are angry you may feel like frowning, shouting or sometimes you can be upset as well. We all get angry sometimes, especially if someone does something that we do not like.

Anger is an emotion that God gave to you, so it is okay to feel angry. He also gave you a gift called self-control which means you have the ability to keep calm when you are angry or upset.

Anytime you are angry, choose to behave well. To do this, you can try the following things:
- Don't shout
- Remember to stay calm
- Walk away and gently talk about what upset you later
- Talk to your mom or dad to help you feel better
- Ask God to help you forgive the person who upset you

My Confession Today

When I am angry I will choose good behaviour.

My Bible Verse

Don't sin by letting anger control you. Don't let the sun go down while you are still angry, for anger gives a foothold to the devil.
Ephesians 4:26-27 (NLT)

You Are Special

30

Before God created the world, He chose you. He loves you so much that He planned everyday of your life before you were born. He decided your looks, the sound of your voice, which family you would be part of, where you would live and who you would become.

God is very, very interested in who you are. He created you especially so that you could live with Him forever.

You are special.

My Confession Today

I am living the good life God planned for me before I was born.

My Bible Verse

For we are God's masterpiece. He has created us anew in Christ Jesus, so we can do the good things he planned for us long ago.
Ephesians 2:10 (NLT)

31 You Have Everything You Need

In this world people need lots of things to live everyday. We need water to stop our thirst, food to eat, clothes to keep us warm in winter, shoes to protect our feet, air to breathe, families to care for us and friends to play with.

God has given all these things to you, but most of all, He wants you to know that He has given you His son, Jesus. Jesus is the only one who can really satisfy your every need. He is the only one that can fill your soul and care for your inner man in a very special way.

There was a man named David in the Bible and when he realised this, he said, 'The Lord is my Shepherd, I have everything I need'. If you have Jesus, then you have everything you need.

My Confession Today

God makes favour and abundance come to me. In Him, I have everything I need.

My Bible Verse

The Lord is my Shepherd; I have all that I need. Psalm 23:1 (NLT)

Wisdom From Above

32

You may not always know what to do, or how to do things. When you find this happens, then you should ask for help.

The best person you can ask for help is God. He promised to give you wisdom when you ask Him for it. He will always give you the heavenly type of wisdom: it's pure, full of peace, gentle, easy to understand and full of good things.

Go on, ask God for help today and then do what He says.

My Confession Today

God helps me by giving me heavenly wisdom.

My Bible Verse

If you need wisdom, ask our generous God, and he will give it to you. He will not rebuke you for asking. But when you ask him, be sure that your faith is in God alone.
James 1: 5-6 (NLT)

33 He's Working In You

There is power working in you right now. Just the same way your heart is pumping blood around your body, the power of God is working in you right now.

When God created you, He planned all the days of your life. He gave His power, which is the Holy Spirit and His word. If you believe and speak God's word, then you have His great ability to make good things happen around you.

My Confession Today

God does more than I can ask by His power that works in me.

My Bible Verse

Now all glory to God, who is able, through his mighty power at work within us, to accomplish infinitely more than we might ask or think.
Ephesians 3: 20 (NLT)

Before Day One

34

No one knows how your bones were formed when you were still growing in your mummy's tummy. No one could see you then, but God could. He formed you by Himself and made you so beautiful in this secret place. He also decided what all the days of your life would be.

Before day one, God made a very good plan for your life!

My Confession Today

I rejoice and thank God for my life.

My Bible Verse

You saw me before I was born. Every day of my life was recorded in your book. Every moment was laid out before a single day had passed.
Psalm 139: 13-16 (NLT)

35 The Purpose of The Book

The Bible is a very special book. It tells a lot of stories that teach you how to live. It tells about people's lives: Abraham, Noah, Joseph, Daniel, David, Ruth, Hannah, Deborah and many others. But the Bible is more than just a story book because everything in it is true.

It especially tells you about the life of Jesus and all the miracles He did. So, when you read your Bible, you must believe that what it says is true. Also believe in Jesus, the Son of God, so that you can have a new life through His name.

My Confession Today

I believe that the Bible is true. I believe in Jesus.

My Bible Verse

The disciples saw Jesus do many other miraculous signs in addition to the ones recorded in this book. But these are written so that you may continue to believe that Jesus is the Messiah, the Son of God, and that by believing in him you will have life by the power of his name.
John 20: 30-31 (NLT)

Into My Heart

36

Do you know that you can have Jesus come into your heart today? It is of great value to ask Him to be your friend.

This is because God loves you so much that He gave His Son's life for you. Many years ago, Jesus was crucified on a cross so that mankind could become friends with God again. He shed His blood as the price that took away all our sins, and now we can live with God forever.

Ask Jesus to come into your heart today.

My Confession Today

Come into my heart Lord Jesus, and wash me clean of sin. Help me to live for you.

My Bible Verse

There is only one God and one Mediator who can reconcile God and humanity - the man Christ Jesus. He gave his life to purchase freedom for everyone. This is the message God gave to the world at just the right time.
1 Timothy 2: 5-6 (NLT)

37 It All Counts

There are so many people on earth and every single one counts. You also count, and everything that you say or do matters. This is why you must choose to be kind and loving to others all the time. Even when someone else hurts you, you can still love.

If you smile at someone, or give a hug, or listen, or shake hands with them, then you are showing love. You can also make sure you don't say bad things about others.

Everything you do or say counts.

My Confession Today

I will love others because love counts. Love holds all things together.

My Bible Verse

Christ is the visible image of the invisible God. He existed before anything else, and he holds all creation together.
Colossians 1: 15 & 17 (NLT)

You Have What You Say

38

You are made in God's image and likeness. This means you are just like Him. You have His ability to make things happen and the Bible calls this creative power.

Each day, say only things that you want to see happen. Good things. The words you speak are full of life and power and they will come to pass for good or for bad. So, choose good.

My Confession Today

I have what I say, so I will say what is right and good.

My Bible Verse

I tell you the truth, you can say to this mountain, 'May you be lifted up and thrown into the sea,' and it will happen. But you must really believe it will happen and have no doubt in your heart.
Mark 11: 23 (NLT)

39 So He Thinks, So Is He

Who are you? Do you know what you want to become when you are older? How about being like God if you learn to think like Him?

The Bible holds God's thoughts and plans for mankind, so the more you read and understand it, the more you become like God. But you must also do what it says to be like Him. Believe that what it says is true and believe that behaving the way it says you should behave is the best way.

Think like God, act like God, be like God.

My Confession Today

God's thoughts are better than mine. I choose to have His thoughts.

My Bible Verse

My thoughts are nothing like your thoughts, says the Lord. And my ways are far beyond anything you could imagine. Just as the heavens are higher than the earth, so my ways are higher than your ways and my thoughts higher than your thoughts.
Isaiah 55: 8-9 (NLT)

Never Thirsty

40

Anytime you are thirsty, you want a drink. This type of drink can only stop your body from being thirsty for a little while. God has provided another source of drink that can quench the thirst and longing of the human soul forever. He did this because He made us spirit, soul and body, and He wants us to be fully satisfied.

When you drink from His well of water, you will never be thirsty again. This well is His Holy Spirit and is the best drink ever.

My Confession Today

As the deer longs for water brooks, my soul waits for God.

My Bible Verse

I thirst for God, the living God.
Psalm 42:2 (NLT)

In His Shadow

Have you ever been afraid of a shadow because it is dark? There really isn't any need to be afraid, you know why?

God has a special shadow and if you stay close to Him and don't leave His side, you will always be protected by His shadow. This means that He will look after you and His presence will be with you all the time. He loves to cover and protect you in His shadow.

My Confession Today

God protects me daily as I stay in His shadow.

My Bible Verse

Those who live in the shelter of the Most High will find rest in the shadow of the Almighty.
Psalm 91:1 (NLT)

Grace

42

Grace is a supernatural ability to do things that you can't do on your own. It is the power to do things well.

Grace is God's gift to you and there is more than enough of it every new day. This means you do not have to use yesterday's grace today because God will give a fresh grace for today.

Grace means trusting and relying on the Holy Spirit to teach you, lead you and help you in life.

Ask God for His grace today.

My Confession Today

Lord, please give me fresh grace every day. Help me to do things well.

My Bible Verse

And the child grew and became strong; he was filled with wisdom, and the grace of God was upon him.
Luke 2:40 (NLT)

43 Talk To God, Listen To Him

Friends are one of the very best things in life. You can talk to them, listen to what they have to say and share things together. If one friend is sad, then the other friend can make them feel better.

God also calls you His friend if you will spend time with Him. When you talk to God every day, ask Him questions and tell Him about your day, but most importantly make sure you listen to what He says in return.

It takes practice listening to God, but you will learn so much by doing this every day.

My Confession Today

When I pray I get closer to God and listen for His direction.

My Bible Verse

The earnest prayer of a righteous person has great power and produces wonderful results.
James 5:16 (NLT)

Super Strength

44

Men and women can do many things; boys and girls too. Did you know that super strength is only made available to you by the Holy Spirit? The Holy Spirit works to produce this type of strength by telling you what God wants. He brings comfort, truth and encouragement. If you are a child of God, He lives constantly in you.

Follow the Holy Spirit by doing what He says so that you will always have super strength.

My Confession Today

I am filled with super strength because I am a child of God. This power is from the Holy Spirit.

My Bible Verse

Through the power of the Spirit you put to death the deeds of your sinful nature, so you will live. For all who are led by the Spirit of God are children of God.
Romans 8:13b-14 (NLT)

45 More Than Enough

God is more than enough. His name is El-Shaddai and it means God Almighty. Since He is your Father, you always have more than enough so that you do not have any needs being unmet. You also have more than enough so that you can share what you have by giving to others.

God made a special promise to make all grace and earthly blessings come to you in abundance. He has also blessed you with all spiritual blessings.

Start today by sharing something with your friends or your siblings.

My Confession Today

The Lord is my Shepherd, I have everything I need.

My Bible Verse

And God will generously provide all you need. Then you will always have everything you need and plenty left over to share with others.
2 Corinthians 9:8 (NLT)

Singing Psalms And Hymns

Singing is a very beautiful thing to do. It sounds wonderful and makes you happy. It also makes those who hear you singing happy.

Singing is one of the ways that you can praise God and tell Him "thank you". The Bible says you should sing psalms and hymns and make melody in your heart to the Lord. It also says that God dwells in the praises of His people.

As you praise God today you will experience His presence with you.

My Confession Today

I love to sing praises to God and bless His holy name.

My Bible Verse

O Lord, our Lord, your majestic name fills the earth! Your glory is higher than the heavens. You have taught children and infants to give you praise, silencing your enemies and all who oppose you.
Psalm 8: 1-2a (NLT)

Give God First Place

The Bible says that Christ died so He may have pre-eminence or the first place. You must always give the first place to God and His word. This shows that you love and honour Him.

You can give Him first place by choosing to obey what you read in your Bible, instead of doing things your own way. You can obey your parents and make sure you do not tell lies or do things that do not please God. You can also spend time praying each day.

When you seek God the most, it means you always want to please Him in every thing you do or say, and He will reward you with a great life.

My Confession Today

I seek first God's way of doing things.

My Bible Verse

The one thing I ask of the Lord - the thing I seek most - is to live in the house of the Lord all the days of my life, delighting in the Lord's perfections and meditating in his Temple.
Psalm 27: 4 (NLT)

Thank You

There are so many awesome things you have in life. Think about it: you have people around who love you, good food to eat, nice clothes to put on, toys to play with and friends to talk to. You can also go for a walk outside or play in the park.

There are a variety of seasons to enjoy: in the summer there are green trees around to provide shade from the warm sun and the breeze blowing gently to keep you cool. In autumn the leaves change their colour and dry out so you can crunch them under your feet. In the winter there is snow or the rain showers. And in the springtime lots of colourful plants come up everywhere.

These are so many reasons to give God thanks. Thank Him today.

My Confession Today

When I think of all the wonderful things around me, I give thanks to the Lord.

My Bible Verse

Therefore let us offer the sacrifice of praise to God continually, that is, the fruit of our lips giving thanks to his name.
Hebrews 13:15 (KJV)

49 I Am Happy And I Know It

How many happy people have you seen today? How could you tell that they were happy?

It is good to show your happiness. When you smile, laugh or are just silently content you show that you are happy and you help to cheer up everybody around you too.

Smile at someone today.

My Confession Today

I love smiling. It shows I am happy and it cheers someone else up.

My Bible Verse

A cheerful heart is good medicine, but a broken spirit saps a person's strength.
Proverbs 17:22 (NLT)

I Want More

50

When you ask politely you get what you asked for. David was a king in the Bible and he asked for more of God. He wanted to live in God's presence and serve Him in His tabernacle. God granted David's request.

Today, ask to receive more of God. Even though you are already created in God's image, there is so much more that you can experience in Him.

My Confession Today

I want more of God.

My Bible Verse

One thing I ask of the LORD, this is what I seek: that I may dwell in the house of the LORD all the days of my life, to gaze upon the beauty of the LORD and to seek him in his temple.
Psalm 27:4 (NIV)

Do You Know Jesus?

The Bible says that when one person repents and comes to Jesus, the angels in heaven rejoice. They have a party!

When Adam and Eve disobeyed God in the Garden of Eden by eating fruit from the tree that they were not supposed to eat from, all of mankind was separated from God, but God sent His Son Jesus to die for you on a cross, so that you could be reconciled back to Him. To be reconciled means that you become a friend of God. This is because He loves you so much. Today, if you have not yet been reconciled back to God, take a bold step and ask Jesus to come into your heart right now. Just pray the prayer below:

**Lord Jesus, I repent of my sins.
Come into my heart.
I make you my Lord and Saviour.
Amen.**

If you have just prayed this prayer, you are now a friend of God. The angels are rejoicing! The Holy Spirit has come to live in your heart and He will lead you each day and show you how to please God and live right. Read your Bible every day to learn about God and walk closely with Him.

Other books now available in the
Hidden Treasure for Little Minds® series:

Conversations With God for 5 to 10 year Olds is a contemporary book of prayers recommended for this age group. Filled with twenty-five different faith-based prayers, it will show your child that they can talk to their loving heavenly Father plainly and expect His answers. It also has some classic conversations like *The Lord's Prayer* and *The Shepherd's Psalm* (Psalm 23), as well as provides a mini-journal section to record answers to prayers or to write out personal conversations.

Your child will find strength, encouragement, safety and direction in the secret place of talking to God and hearing Him speak.

Other books coming soon in the Hidden Treasure for Little Minds® series:

Standing Tall, Living Strong: An Activity Book for 5 to 10 year Olds
Your 5 to 10 year old will have fun completing the activities in this workbook. It is designed to teach values like love, patience and a can-do attitude in an enjoyable way. It contains puzzles, think-through tasks, find-the-verse exercises, match the story to the names, memory training and much more. The activities can be used to capture family time with other siblings and parents.

Daily Devotions for 7 to 10 year Olds
This is a follow on from the Daily Devotions for 2 to 6 year olds book that lasts the whole year through. In addition to weekly themes, it contains simple memory verses and prayers, a daily notes column, end-of-week study reviews and a mini-journal section. It is aimed at building your child's personal faith in God and helping him or her develop a deeper love for spending quality time alone in God's presence

About the Author

Adesola Obunge received a Bachelor of Science (Honours) degree in Chemistry from the University of St Andrews in Scotland and she is also a Chartered Scientist and Chartered Chemist. Currently engaged in International Regulatory Affairs and Policy within the Pharmaceutical Industry, she is author of various science articles published in professional journals and she loves mentoring secondary school children; giving talks about how they can go on to pursue and enjoy science-related careers.

Besides this, Adesola enjoys writing inspirational articles and poems which are published in Christian magazines. She is also a worship leader at her local church.

Adesola and her husband live in London (England) with their two children.

To find out more about Adesola Obunge and her books, see www.adesolaobunge.com

All her titles are available for purchase at all good book stores, and online at Amazon.co.uk, Barnes & Noble, Christianbook.com, www.adesolaobunge.com and at the Authorhouse.co.uk online bookstore.

About the Illustrator

As a graduate from the Art's University College at Bournemouth, Jonathan Harper offers designs with personality and innovation, all developed by thinking outside the box.

Although Jonathan's field of work is in graphic design, his first love is illustration. He draws influence from every style that is available, and can adapt his skills to fit the brief of the client.

Jonathan specialises in creating identities for businesses. He is also experienced with design for print, as well as web design.

You can contact him at ojharper@googlemail.com or view his website at http://www.ojharper.co.uk